Surprised

BY

Grace

MARIE CAMPBELL

ISBN 979-8-89043-427-2 (paperback)
ISBN 979-8-89043-428-9 (digital)

Christian Faith Publishing
832 Park Avenue
Meadville, PA 16335
www.christianfaithpublishing.com

Printed in the United States of America

Marie has written her story with a genuineness and transparencey that touches the heart. Her faith in God as Savior and Lord is a consistent theme providing both the strength and hope to traverse various challenges experienced. Her writing can be a treasure and inspiration to family and friends.

Kay C. Bruce, PsyD
Counselor and Chaplain

Marie Campbell has written an honest and thought provoking book. It takes a great deal of courage to be honest about the shadowy things in one's life but she shows how a great God has it well in hand. I have seen her struggles and I pray that this book and the help it will give others, brings a settled sense to her soul. I know that she has personally helped me with wise counsel at times and I am grateful. I believe this book can offer hope to others who have and are walking a dark path, hope that no matter their situation or hardship, God can use them. Also, that there is no past that God cannot redeem.

Pastor Steve Nute
Nealley's Corner Church
Hampden, Maine

Marie Campbell has written a book bearing her soul about her past dark days in a very vivid language. If you are struggling, you will be able to relate. The great part of her stories are the truth that Jesus stays with us even when we can't grasp it. She shares how light shines through and her life does get better. I can highly recommend this book, especialy to those in a dark place, but also to those ones doing well, because it will cause you to appreciate your life even more.

Reverend Richard A. Berry
Senior Pastor
Shelters by Jesus

This is a story of resilience, When life's circumstances feel as if we can't go on, we find that God is right there showing us the way. Marie captured the essence of what resilience means as she details all the ways God showed up in expected and unexpected ways. Her story is an inspiration to the depths of the human spirit and of a God who never let's go of our hand.

Michele A. Lewis
Author, 'Confessions of a feel good addict'

Mom

Where do I begin? I suppose at the beginning in order to give a little background. Mom and Dad had a beautiful baby girl in 1942. Nola Corrine, my only sister. She would soon become a big sister to brother Harvey when she was two years old and then three more times to three more brothers, Richard, Joel and Paul. In her teen years, she was a significant help to Mom, as she routinely cared for her four brothers. Being the eldest and Mom needing help, she was forced to grow up fast. The next two pregnancies turned into home miscarriages. Mom told me that both were boys.

On December 29, 1957, Dad came home from the hospital to announce to Nola, who was now fifteen years old, that she finally got the sister she wanted. She would not believe it until Dad took her to the hospital to hold her little sister: me.

Mom had wanted another girl, and she trusted that God would answer her prayer. She told me this story and how excited she was when I was born. She said, "You are the answer to my prayer, and you are a miracle." She told me that her pregnancy with me was difficult and then dangerous. She was bedridden for the last three months to prevent another miscarriage. My siblings have always teased me about being Mom's favorite. Sixty-three years later, the teasing continues. That's all right because I do accept that God answered Mom's prayer.

Due to the significant age differences in my older siblings, I did not have the blessing of growing up with them. My sister was getting married when I was three years old, and my three older brothers were off to active duty in the army and air force. I really only remember growing up with my youngest brother, Paul. He was five years older than me. We had the typical older brother–younger sister relationship. I was usually bugging him, and he was usually irritated with me.

Mostly what I remember about my childhood is that I felt very safe and loved by my mother. She was very expressive in communicating her love for me with words and deeds. Mom was a hugger, and that always let me know that I was wanted, safe, and loved. My childhood memories do not become clear for me until around the age of eight. To this day, I do not understand the reason for that. I only have a dim memory of when I was five years old and Mom made me a pink-and-white striped dress and put a big bow in my hair for a picture. I remember her saying, "Smile big." I tried so hard to smile big that I tilted my head sideways. I was also frustrated with the effort, and my tight-lipped expression made that clear. I still have that dress. Just can't seem to part with it. Memories can be so powerful.

Some of my favorite early childhood memories included the giant bonfires that Dad would build and then Mom would let us cook our dinner in. Sometimes it was hotdogs, and other times it was meat and vegetables wrapped in tinfoil and set on the coals to cook. Of course, dessert was s'mores!

Another was of climbing the trees in our yard. We had apple trees, cherry trees, plum trees, an apricot tree, and a grapevine. We also had a large evergreen in the front yard that I climbed. The fruit trees always came in handy when I got hungry before dinnertime. I still remember eating little green apples until I had a stomachache. My favorite tree was the tallest cherry tree. At the top, it branched off into three directions. One of the directions had three smaller branches that formed a perfect seat for me. I would straddle the branches, and I found it quite comfortable. To make it a little more exciting, I would lean forward and backward, as if on a swing, to get the entire branch swaying. Apparently, that was dangerous. My mom opened the kitchen window and hollered out, "You be careful up there, young lady." To this day I still giggle at that because I had no idea I was in any danger; I was just having the time of my life in my favorite spot.

I remember how I would watch the birds land on the branches near me. They were chirping away, and I was enthralled with them. I would talk to them and sing to them. I just made up the words to what my little heart was feeling. I was sure they understood me, and I was transported into a wonderful world where something magical was happening. I still recall the butterflies in my stomach as I felt the excitement of having this special relationship with the birds. My early childhood was safe and happy.

I was the last child and was the one that, by medical standards, did not have a good chance of survival. Her doctor told her not to get pregnant again because she had miscarried two babies. My mom told him in no uncertain terms, "God promised me another little girl." The doctor said that if she got pregnant again, she needed to find herself another doctor. He was done with her. The promise from God that Mom was convinced of and my arrival after a difficulty pregnancy created the foundations for the strong relationship that my mother and I would grow to know.

Up until I turned fourteen, my mom and I enjoyed each other and got along very well. We spent time cooking, baking, sewing, and playing with our animals, just to name a few of the things we did together. My life was safe and fun. My overarching memory is that I was happy.

It was as clear as if it were yesterday. In the summer of my fourteenth year, I became a selfish and rebellious brat. I began to keep company with peers that had behaviors that would prove to be detrimental to me. I had been raised in a Christian home where I was taught about God and that Jesus died for my sins, that he rose from the grave, and is alive and active. I was taught to believe in Him and ask Him to be my Savior, which I did when I was eight years old. My mother knelt by her bedside with me and led me in a prayer that changed my life. All of a sudden I was fourteen and rejecting everything I had been taught. I became determined to do whatever I decided was right for me, and I didn't care what my parents or anyone else thought. I set out on a self-destructive path for the next six years.

Heartbreak

My girlfriend asked me to meet her and her boyfriend at the fair. She was setting me up with a friend of her boyfriend. I was fourteen. As I approached them, I was evaluating the physical looks of not only the guy that was meant for me but her boyfriend as well. The guy for me was average-looking. Her boyfriend was tall, dark, and very handsome. I had butterflies in my stomach when I saw him. This feeling was very much hormonal and emotional and extremely powerful.

In the secrecy of my thoughts, I had decided that her boyfriend would one day be mine. I was so determined in my mind that as the night continued, and it came time to kiss, I had the nerve to ask my girlfriend if I could kiss her boyfriend instead of the date she had set me up with. She actually agreed. That was the beginning of a nightmare for me that I mistakenly considered as the best thing that had ever happened for me. Throughout the next six years, I routinely drank alcohol, smoked cigarettes and marijuana, took speed, lied, and had a constant focus on a physical relationship with this guy. I lost my virginity in the summer of my fifteenth year.

Due to my irregular menstruation cycle, I did not become pregnant until I was nineteen years old. I was terrified. I knew in my heart that this guy I had been with since I was fourteen was not interested in becoming a father. I knew he was a cheater and was only interested in pleasing himself. Even knowing all this, I kept telling myself that I would change him. I still held some hope, although it was so very slight, that he would determine to do the right thing and stay with me, and eventually marry me.

With great fear in my heart, I told him that I was pregnant. I felt that the right thing to do was to tell him. His response was not what I longed for. He became angry. He asked me to get an abortion. He rejected me. I should not have been surprised. Even though I had known his character for many years, I was still devastated. I remember thinking how I thought that eventually he would grow to love me and want to marry me. *That* never happened. My greatest fear became reality, and my entire world fell apart.

I had yet to tell my mom and dad. I still see the tears in their eyes. I still hear the sorrow in their voices and see the sadness on their faces. They were heartbroken. Although this was so painful for them to hear, they did not reject me. They told me they would help me through this. It was a great comfort to me to have my parents help me at this time in my life when I was scared and mourning the loss of the person that I honestly felt I loved and wanted to spend the rest of my life with. As I write this, I am now sixty-five years old. My advice to parents is to have crucial conversations with their daughters on their value and to not be quick to give their heart away. I had given my heart away to a person whose behavior was extremely damaging for me.

My Christian upbringing taught me that abortion was wrong. It was a sin. I couldn't bring myself to do it. I felt trapped. I didn't want to have the baby without him, and I didn't want to get an abortion. I sank into depression, and my drinking and drug use increased. I was working as a housekeeper at a local hotel at this time in my life. I had lots of alone time while cleaning the rooms to think about my situation and my future. I cried a lot. I became fearful that I was not ready to be a mother and that nobody in the future would want to marry someone who already had a child. I felt myself sinking into despair.

While at work one day, I bent over to tuck in the sheets on a bed and I felt a sudden, sharp pain, and a gush of blood saturated my pants. I called my mom, and she took me to the emergency room. My body was in the process of aborting the baby. The doctor told me the baby was dead and had to be removed. The doctor performed a

D&C, which is a procedure of dilating the cervix to enter the uterus and scrape out the contents. The contents were my dead baby.

My mom went through the hell of my behavior throughout my teen years. She never made me feel like a bad person. She never rejected me. She never gave up on me. She always tried to encourage me and listen to me whenever I needed to talk. She demonstrated the love of Jesus to me that I did not deserve and desperately needed. Without her, it is highly likely that I would not be writing my story. She was an anchor of hope when I had none. She loved me when I hated myself.

Over time, I was able to confess my sinful ways to God and recommit my life to Him. With God's power, my behavior changed. I stopped seeking satisfaction and fulfillment in the selfish ways of the world and began to seek living a life by God's values. God was faithful to heal me through this time, and he gave my dad and mom the grace to forgive me.

From that time, at the age of nineteen, up until the earthly death of Mom, we remained close in our relationship. I say we went through hell together and came out friends on the other side. She was the one who demonstrated the love of Christ to me and never gave up on me. This created an ever-stronger bond than we had experienced before. We enjoyed one another's company. We cherished our times together and the joy of encouraging one another in our faith walk with Jesus. We would laugh and cry, work and play, and would have the most wonderful conversations about life.

I was able to share openly with Mom about what I was thinking and feeling. I knew I was safe in her love for me. She loved me enough that when my thoughts and behaviors were not pleasing to the Lord, she would gently, yet firmly, correct me. I highly valued that I was safe in my relationship with my mom. The example of God's love that my mom demonstrated to me impacted me powerfully all my life, especially when I was the most difficult to deal with. The person that I am today was shaped by God's powerful love through my mom who relied on God to be enough for not only herself but enough for me too.

God called Mom home on January 26, 2009, a few minutes after 5:00 a.m. To this day, in the year 2022, I still think of her often and miss her intensely. I find that when I am going through difficult times in my life, I long for more of the unconditional love and acceptance that she demonstrated to me. I miss our meaningful conversations. I miss her advice. I miss that little smirk of a smile on her face that let me know she was once again going to give me some sound advice, usually with a heap of, "Now, Marie, your attitude is not good, and you need to trust God." She was always right about that. She loved me enough to tell it like it was, and it was counsel that was straight from God's Word. My mom's commitment and example of following God in her life was powerful in shaping mine. Now, when I go through times of struggle or pain, I still hold in my heart the words she said to me, and I find that they are still the counsel that I need.

There is another chapter about Mom that I want to share with you. It is the incredible time with her just a short nine hours before God called her home. I'll tell you all about this miraculous time that God gave her and me in another chapter.

Our Beginning

I was nineteen years old when I met a guy who was very different from all the other guys I had known. He was kind and thoughtful; I wasn't used to that. He was a Christian too. It sounds so stupid to say this, but it was true; he treated me with kindness and respect, and that made me uncomfortable. I had not been treated with kindness and respect in my previous relationship. I had become so used to it that I didn't see how damaging it was until Doug came along and demonstrated the opposite behavior to me. The way he treated me with thoughtfulness really shed a light on the darkness in which I was living.

I still remember how Doug's kindness to me gave me a mental jolt that caused me to wake up and see how my choices had engulfed me in a life of danger, fear, pain, and sorrow. You would have thought that nobody would have wanted to live like that and would have noticed how heartbreaking a life it was, but I had become so numb to God's promptings and comfortable with living in my sinful pattern that I just kept on doing it.

Even after all these years, it still brings tears to my eyes when I recall my foolishness. I convinced myself that although my lifestyle was an awful mess, it was what I deserved. I had reasoned that Doug offered me a relationship that was too good for me. I recall telling him one day, "You're a really nice guy, and you deserve a nice girl. And I'm not her." That statement pretty much sums up what I thought of myself. It is not surprising that after my repeated efforts to discourage Doug from pursuing me, he finally decided to give up.

Weeks passed and he did not call or stop by where I was living with my parents. I found myself missing him. The missing him quickly translated into longing to see him again. I experienced an overwhelming emptiness because he was no longer a part of my life. I remember thinking what a fool I was to turn away from a guy that had treated me so well.

One day, I accidently crossed paths with the girl who was dating his friend. I asked her to please tell her boyfriend to have Doug call me. He called me. What he said made my heart sink. He said, "I don't have time to come and see you. I'm getting out of the navy and going home." In May of 1978, he went home: clear across the United States to Maine.

We wrote letters and talked on the phone about once a week. Doug decided that I was worth him making a trip cross-country to come and see me, and that amazed me. He rode a bus for several days to come out and visit me in June of 1978. I was so excited to see him, and I quickly found myself settling into a place of comfort when I was with him. I enjoyed Doug's humor and kindness. I was growing in love with Doug.

After a couple weeks, it was time for him to head back to Maine. Saying goodbye to him was very hard for me. Doug asked me to come to Maine to meet his family. He said, "I'm going to warn you. If you come to Maine, I'm going to ask you to marry me." I saved for the airfare and in September of 1978, I flew to Maine to meet his family.

When we walked into the New England farmhouse, his mom and dad were waiting for us at the small table in the kitchen. They were so warm and welcoming that I immediately felt comfortable with them. After dinner one night, Doug asked me if I'd like to take a walk with him down to the river. As we began to make our way through the woods, Doug stepped into a hole and hurt his leg. He insisted that with the use of a stick as a crutch, he could keep going, so we continued to work our way down to the river. We sat on a huge rock by the side of the Penobscot river. I still recall the way Doug asked me to marry him. He said, "So do you think you could spend the rest of your life here?"

I answered him immediately, "Yes, I think I can."

After dinner the next night, Doug announced to his family that we were getting married. He went to the calendar on the wall and asked me what I thought would be a good day. We agreed on November 18, 1978. His grandmother exclaimed, "Nobody gets married in November!"

Doug said, "Well, that just confirmed it. November 18 it is!" I flew home and had about eight weeks to plan our wedding. It all came together very quickly, and I was extremely pleased with the plan.

Doug flew back to Washington State from Maine. It was so wonderful for me that Pastor John Durkee was available to perform our wedding ceremony. We were off to Oregon for our honeymoon. Being the romantic that I was, I had asked God for snow on our wedding day. I had not taken into consideration that it could likely make our travel difficult. It started snowing the moment that Pastor Durkee introduced us to the congregation as Mr. and Mrs. Douglas Campbell. My attendant ran up to me, pointed out the glass front doors, and shouted, "Look! It's snowing. It started coming down the minute he introduced you." It continued to come down so heavily that the interstate was closed and we were not able to get to our desired location. Nevertheless, we enjoyed the beauty of the snow and were joyful to be married.

The plan all along was that we would live in Maine. Three days after the wedding, we were on a plane to Maine. I can still remember sitting on the plane and thinking to myself, *What have you done?* You see, I had never been farther than Idaho, and that was only for one weekend. I always stayed close to home, hung around with the same people, and went to the same places. Now I was off to a new way of life, and yes, I was scared!

We settled into life in Maine with a rental home not far from his parents' and with jobs. There was so much that felt strange to me. I felt out of place. I grew homesick. One day on the phone with my mom, I told her that I wanted to come home. She lovingly said to me, "Honey, you need to grow where you are planted." I knew she was right, but the struggle stayed with me.

I thank God for the wise-and-loving advice of my mom which God used to help me to be willing to trust Him as I adjusted to a new life. And I thank you, God, for the wise-and-loving advice of my mother-in-law. You will hear more about her in the next chapter.

A Special Blessing

When I moved to Maine three days after we were married, I found myself extremely homesick. Everything and everyone was new to me. I did not have the comfort of the familiarity and being physically close to my mom. It is sad to say this, but it is the truth: I felt very alone in this new place. It was an experience that not even my new husband could fully understand. He was surrounded with his family, so he was having an opposite experience of what I was having. He had missed them greatly while he was in service; however, that all melted away, as he was now home.

It was me that was away from my family. I'd never gone this far from home. I'd never been away from my family. I had a new husband and a new family to get to know. I had new surroundings and needed to learn my way around. I knew God was with me, and yet the sadness seemed to close in on me like a heavy blanket that was choking me. I still remember that conversation with my mom in which she told me I needed to grow where I was planted. I knew she was right, but every fiber in me just wanted to run home!

My mother-in-law would become a blessing that I didn't see coming. I don't remember exactly how it came about in the beginning, but from the very start, I called her Mom. It was when our water pipes in our rental house froze that the blessing would begin to unfold. The house we rented had poor insulation. It was so cold in that house that the water in the toilet froze one night! We moved into the large New England farmhouse with Mom and Dad. This provided the opportunity for Mom and me to spend more time together. We would work in the kitchen together and have the best time. I grew to love her more every day. I realized that she was the gift from God that I needed to help me through a very difficult time.

In February of 1979, I became pregnant. I continued to work at the shoe factory. I was careful to not lift any bundles of leather so as to protect my body and the baby during this time. My job, as one who cut the leather pieces that would become shoes, required that I stand to operate the machine. I had two breaks and a lunchtime that provided the opportunity for me to rest.

One day, as I was standing at the machine, I had a sudden gush that saturated my pants. I didn't know what was happening or why, but I knew that something was very wrong. I was scared. I didn't know what to do. I went into the bathroom. When another gal came in, I asked her to please go get the secretary because something was wrong. She ran and got her. I told her I was pregnant and that I think my water broke. I gave her directions to our home so someone could go tell Doug what was happening. We had no house phone and no cell phones at the time. Doug worked nights, so he was at home, sleeping.

The next thing I remember was being put on a stretcher and taken by ambulance to the hospital. Doug soon arrived. I signed a lot of papers, giving the medical staff permission to treat me. One medication in particular was still considered experimental. The purpose of this medication was to mature the baby's lungs. I was told it needed twenty-four hours to work. I remember telling them that I would try to hold off. A little humor was needed at the time because I was really scared!

Our son's story is shared in another chapter. What I want to tell you about is how my relationship with Doug's mom deepened while we lived with them. We had some great conversations about Jesus and our relationship with him. She was an encourager. The day came that it was time to bring our son home from the hospital. After three and a half months in the hospital, he had finally reached the goal of at least five pounds. That was the requirement before they would let us take him home. He was actually five pounds and two ounces! I remembered significant details like this. We wrapped him warmly in his homecoming outfit. It was December 23, 1979.

My husband had a wonderful surprise for me. One day I was in the living room, sitting by the woodstove. Doug asked me to let him hold our son. Then he asked me to take a few steps to the side and stop. I had no idea what he was doing. Then he had me close my eyes, and he asked me to sit down. I found myself relaxing in a beautiful antique rocking chair! I cried. He was so sweet to give me and our son a special place to be together. By the way, I still have that chair.

I had no idea how to be a mother, and because our son was born three months prematurely, weighing only one lb. and fifteen oz., I felt like he was very fragile. One day, he was crying. He cried for about two hours. Actually, it turned into more of a scream. I came downstairs and found Mom in the kitchen. I was crying. I said, "I need help, Mom! I don't know what's wrong with him or what to do." You see, before we brought our baby home, Mom told me that she did not want to interrupt our lives. She told me that she was available anytime I needed her but that I needed to ask her for help. She had experienced seven children of her own, so she knew how to care for babies. Oh, on top of that, she had been an LPN.

Mom reached out and took our son in her arms. She said that she thought it may be that he was not able to have a bowel movement and needed some help. We went upstairs, where she prepared a solution of warm water and a little dish soap. She took the rubber bulb (usually used to clear the nose), sucked up a little of the solution, and continued to give him an enema. It was very quick that he released his bowels, and all of a sudden, just like that, he stopped crying. That was it. He needed that. I would have never known how to help him. I was so grateful that we were living with Mom and Dad so that I could learn from her how to care for our son. Mom Campbell and I would share many hours together of grocery shopping, of cooking, of great conversations, and of me learning from her how to best care for my son.

In May of 1980, we moved back to Washington State. The closeness I had enjoyed with Mom Campbell came to an end. It was hard to say goodbye to her. For the next forty-plus years, we lived away. We made visits every couple years or so, and those were always great times. At each trip, Mom and Dad Campbell enjoyed seeing how their grandson was growing.

On one of our visits, Mom was in a nursing home due to a fall and a broken hip. She also had dementia trying to take a hold of her. It was difficult to see her this way because she was a caregiver of others, always busy loving others. Now here she was, not able to go anywhere except from the bed to a chair in the nursing home. She never complained, although she had difficult challenges that restricted her desire to be caring for others. This is the blessing that God blessed me with: a mother-in-law who became another mom to me, a friend, a teacher, an encourager, and one who loved me deeply. She helped me through one of the most challenging times in my life, and because of that, I learned, as my mom would say, "Grow where I was planted."

This visit was different from all other visits. I felt in my soul that it would be the last with Mom Campbell. I was wrestling with how to express my deepest love, respect, and gratefulness to her for how she loved me. I recalled the chorus to a song that communicated what I felt. I told Mom that I would not punish her with my singing. I knelt beside her chair and quoted the words to this chorus: "Thank you for giving to the Lord. I am a life that was changed. Thank you for giving to the Lord. I am so glad you gave." I kissed her on the cheek and told her I loved her. She gave me that beautiful smile of hers and squeezed my hands, which were holding hers. God knew I needed Mom Campbell. I can honestly tell you that had she not been there for me, I truly believe that I would have given up and run back home. But God had me covered.

From Broken to Healed

As far as I knew, life was going well for us. We had moved back to Washington State because employment options were much better. We were settled in an apartment; we were both working and had our wonderful son. Doug was also attending the local community college. He was the president of the student body and was very popular.

Now for the broken part. Reliving this story is painful. It was like being caught in a nightmare that I could not stop. Doug came home from work one day, as usual, but it quickly became evident to me that something was not right. I needed to know what was wrong, so I pushed him for an answer. He kept telling me to not keep asking. I continued to push until the words I heard were words that completely devastated me. He said, "I don't love you. I never have, and I never will." Those words were seared on my heart. I couldn't believe what I heard. This was the beginning of the end, and I felt completely lost, confused, and hopeless. The man who had pursued me just told me I was nothing to him. My world fell apart.

It wasn't long before he moved out. The next two years were a living hell. I kept working and doing my best to care of our son. I hated that every corner of the apartment reminded me of my now-broken life, so I quickly found another place to rent. I remember having chest pains and seeing a heart specialist. He told me that my heart was very healthy and that what I was experiencing was stress. I cried a lot. To this day, I don't know how I was able to function enough to keep working. All I can say is that God was carrying me.

I continued attending the church where we had met. I had a friendship with a gal who met with me weekly to pray with me. She was wonderful, a godsend. Every weekend I either went to my mom and dad's home or my sister's. The weekends were my time to find the support and love that I needed.

One day mom was visiting me at my place. While she was there, Doug called. He asked me to meet him at the park that was near my place because he wanted to talk to me. I hung up in shock. My mom asked, "Well, what did he say?" I shared the conversation with her. I told her I was so confused and scared; I was sure he was going to hand me divorce papers. My mom asked me to sit down next to her. She took my hands in hers and looked me in the eyes as she said, "Now what have we been praying for? Go meet him, and I will stay and watch my grandson."

I was sick with fear as I walked down the pier to meet Doug. I didn't say a word. He began, "I don't know if you can ever forgive me..." He asked me to give him another chance. He asked me if he could come home. I was so afraid. He had completely broken my trust. Honestly, I was numb. The pain I had suffered for so long had severely damaged me, and I questioned if I had what it would take to try. I didn't know if I could ever trust him again. Have I mentioned how difficult it is to tell this part of my story? I could continue to tell specifics of the pain I experienced; however, I am not going to do that. You can know this: I became so depressed that I was considering taking my own life. That pretty much sums up my broken world.

I am now going to share with you what the power of God did for us. It was not an instant healing. It was slow, and it was hard. We both had hurt one another deeply. The brick walls we had put up had to come down one brick at a time. It is not easy to trust once trust has been broken. I was full of fear, and I begged God to help me because I wasn't sure I could do this.

Doug moved back in. I had lived without him for more than two years. I wanted him home and at the same time it felt strange to have him home. This is what I had asked God for, but I worried about what to talk about and how to act around him. I remember constantly wondering if I was going to be enough for him this time. Was I saying things right? Was I acting right? Was it going to be all right, or would he leave again? I prayed a lot. I cried a lot. I felt awkward a lot. The thought kept going through my mind, *I wasn't enough for him in the first place. How am I going to be enough for him now?* I was still me, and he threw me away. I was consumed with fear that he would reject me again, and I didn't think I could take that.

We began attending a different church, Crossroads Neighborhood church. I was comfortable with it because I was raised attending a CMA church, and that is what this church was; so it was familiar to me. We agreed that we felt comfortable there. We stayed for many years and enjoyed the friendships that we built there. I enjoyed helping in Sunday school, and Doug enjoyed helping in the youth group.

As time went on, I joined the deaconess group, and Doug served on the governing board. We continued to grow in our faith and in our relationship. We had learned that rather than looking to one another to be our everything, we needed to both be looking to Jesus to be our everything. We were facing in the same direction. Following God's way for our lives and our marriage changed us. God heard my cry. He was healing me, Doug, and our relationship. God was showing us daily that He could be trusted to heal, to hold us, and to teach us that with Him as the foundation of our marriage, we would experience real love.

God continued giving us His strength to remove those brick walls, to be willing to try to trust again, and to let Him be our foundation and the source of love in our marriage. We have been blessed by God with many years of wonderful times together. We have received nurturing and encouraging from family, friends, and wonderful teachers and pastors throughout the years. We have been blessed with the opportunity to be involved with many ministries over the years in the churches we have attended. Some of these ministries included being Sunday school leaders, youth staff, leading the young married group, being part of the drama group at church, and going on a short-term missions trip to Africa.

As we continued to grow in the Lord individually and in our marriage, God has given us the strength to stay focused on Him and His leading in our future. I will share with you more adventures that God provided as we trusted Him to teach us how to forgive, trust, and love one another more deeply than we ever thought was possible. That is when the great adventures began. Stay tuned.

Aaron

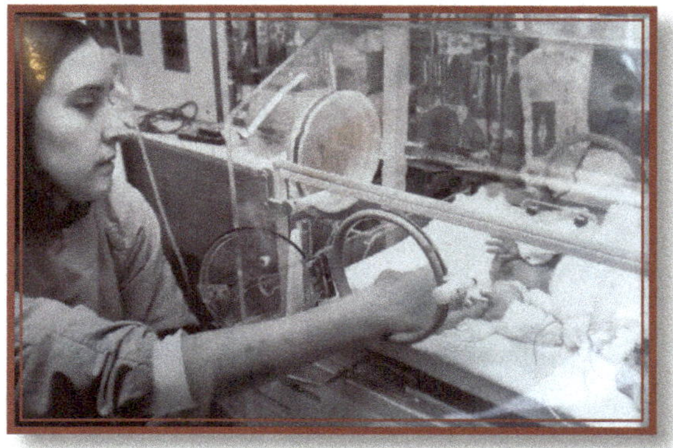

Sometimes it seems like yesterday. I was just living the good life; loving my new husband, Doug; and looking forward to wonderful adventures together. Within the first few months, I became pregnant.

It was just another day for me at work. I worked the day shift in the shoe factory. Because Doug worked nights at Kenworth Trucking Company, he was at home, sleeping. This was in 1979, and we didn't have cell phones in those early days. In fact, we didn't even have a house phone.

I was standing at my cutting station when all of a sudden my water broke. I panicked. I ran to the bathroom. I am thankful to God that within seconds of me entering the bathroom, another gal entered. I said, "I need help. I'm pregnant, and something is wrong. Go get the secretary in the office." I told her that my husband was at home, but we did not have a phone; so I gave her directions to our house, and she sent someone to tell Doug what was happening.

He did not answer the door, so the employee knocked on the bedroom window. Doug told me she was yelling, "Your wife is having a baby!" He told me later that he thought he was dreaming. He quickly realized it was for real and was up, fast, and on his way to the hospital.

I remember a lot of activity around me: medical people moving quickly and lots of terminology I didn't understand. All I knew was that something was very wrong, and I couldn't stop it. To this day I do not know how many papers I signed, but one in particular I still remember. It gave the doctor's permission to use a drug on me that was considered experimental. They told me it was to delay labor and help mature the baby's lungs rapidly, but it needed a minimum of twenty-four hours to work. I lay there for several hours as they monitored me. The drug slowed my labor for a few hours, but then the labor pains started again. The doctor explained to me that it was critical to get me to Portland, Maine, as quickly as possible to give my baby the best chance of survival.

It was an emergency ambulance ride with lights flashing the entire way from Bangor to Portland. Doug was exhausted. He rode up front. His oldest brother, Bud, was a nurse at the Bangor hospital. He came to see me as soon as he heard I was there. When it came time for the ambulance ride, Bud asked me if I wanted him to ride with me. I was so comforted by that, and although there was already another nurse in the ambulance, Bud got in too. He talked to me and had me explain to him what I was feeling. It was such a blessing to have him with me.

It was the worst weather day of the year. There was thunder and lightning and heavy rain the entire way to Portland Maine Medical Center. I would soon learn that this hospital was one of the top ten in the US for premature babies at that time.

The doctor examined me and placed a probe on the baby's head to monitor the heart rate. With every labor pain, the heart rate of the baby grew faster and louder. I remember the doctor saying, "This baby is a fighter. This baby is coming." Then he said, "This baby has a fifty-fifty chance."

I responded immediately with, "He'll be okay." The doctor asked me how I knew the baby was a boy. I told him, "I know because I asked God for a boy with blond hair and blue eyes."

He simply responded, "Oh, okay. Here we go."

The nurse asked me if my husband was going into the delivery room with me. I laughed and said, "Oh, no, I don't think so. We were planning on taking the Lamaze class, but he isn't prepared for this."

Her response was, "Well, you have to go in, so I think he should go in too." The next time I saw Doug, he was all suited up and ready to go into the delivery room. I was laughing in between contractions.

Bright lights, several suited-up medical people, my husband, and a large mirror is what I remember. Doug held my left hand, and I held the grip with my right hand. After my first push, the doctor walked up to my face, leaned in, and said, "This baby is not breathing. I need you to really push right now!" With my next push, our son with blond hair (what little he had) and blue eyes entered the world. Remember that drug I told you about that was to help mature his lungs; the drug that needed twenty-four hours to work? Well, Aaron was born approximately twenty-five hours after they gave me that drug.

I tried to sit up and look, but the medical team stepped in front of the mirror to block my view. Our son was dark blue because he was not breathing. They didn't want me to see him like that, but I caught a glimpse of him as they moved him to a table. Doug let go of my hand and walked over to see our baby. He told me later that as he looked at him, he thought that would be the last time he saw him. He felt he was saying goodbye to our son. The medical team worked to get him breathing, and once he was stabilized, they took him right to the preemie nursery.

The head nurse, Mrs. Poore, attempted to prepare me for what I would see the first time I entered the preemie nursery. There was a poster outside the nursery which read, "Please be patient. God is not finished with me yet." What a precious way to encourage the mothers who would enter that room, wondering, while staring at their tiny baby, if they would live.

I will always remember the first time I walked into that room. I followed Mrs. Poore as she escorted me to the incubator in which Aaron lay. He had an oxygen tube in his nose. He had pads adhered to his tiny, bony chest and wires that connected to the heart monitor. He had a bandage on his heel where a blood sample had been taken. The machines made pumping and beeping sounds. He was so little, just one pound and fifteen ounces! I froze in place and just stared at him. I felt a wave of sadness drown me. Like all the other mothers who had babies in that room, I wondered if he would live. I begged God, "Please let him live. And if you know that you are going to take him, please take him soon before I keep falling in love with him more and more and getting my hopes up." That was the plea of my heart. I felt incredibly helpless. I was in shock. I was afraid. I was the saddest I've ever been in my life! I begged God every day, many times a day, to let our son live.

Mrs. Poore was such a blessing during this time. I will always remember her sweet, gentle way of encouraging me to keep talking to Aaron, to keep touching him, to keep saving my breast milk so he could have the best nourishment possible. And most importantly, to remember that God was not done with my son. Although Mrs. Poore and I never had a personal conversation about faith, I am convinced that I will see her in heaven because her life emanated the fruit of the Spirit.

I was blessed with being able to live with Mom Campbell's cousin in Portland so I could be close to the hospital. I went to be with Aaron twice a day for the two months he was in the hospital. I would open the door of the incubator and put my little finger in the palm of his hand. He would wiggle and turn his head toward me as I spoke to him. *That* was awesome!

My mom and dad were in Washington State and couldn't afford to come and be with me. To be as engaged as they could, Mom would write regularly and ask me to read her words to Aaron. What a joy that was for me. Then one day Mom mailed a small music box, a piano that played "The Entertainer" by Scott Joplin. The first time I played it for Aaron, he wiggled and his heart rate increased. He arched himself from his head to his heels and turned toward the open door of the incubator where I held the music box. It was a special time, as Aaron was engaging with me and the music. It became a regular practice for us every time I was with him.

Is it any wonder that when Aaron was seven years old, for his first piano recital, he chose to play that very song? I had never told him that I played that little music box for him while he was in the hospital. Amazing, right? Well, all I have to say about that is that God is amazing!

Doug came down from Bangor every weekend. His company was very good to us. Understanding our challenge with being apart during this difficult time in our life, they allowed Doug to alter his schedule. They also paid him to drive the Kenworth trucks between the Bangor and Portland shops. Those two months that Aaron was in the Portland hospital were very hard on us. Being separated from one another every Monday through Friday was so difficult. I know that God collected the tears that I cried.

One day the doctor asked to talk with us. He informed us that Aaron's eyes were showing signs of damage from the pure oxygen he had to have for the first twenty-four hours of life, which was a must to give him a chance of survival. My heart sank as I heard the words, "It can cause total and irreversible blindness." I cried out to God with a pain that I had never experienced before. I wept harder than I knew was possible.

In the midst of my heartache, God spoke to me. It was not with audible words. It was His Spirit ministering to my spirit with amazing clarity. God said, *Don't ask me to heal Aaron's eyes. Praise me that I've already done it.* Now here I am, a twenty-one-year-old receiving a message directly from God. At this point in my life, I had never had God talk to me like this. Although I didn't fully understand it, I knew it was God, and I knew it was right. I knew it was from God and not my own thinking because I certainly did not think this way.

I needed some hugs from family, so I rode back home with Doug on one of his weekend trips. The Bible study that met in Gram Campbell's home consisted of a gathering of family and dear friends, about thirty-five people or so. It was so wonderful to be home and to receive so many hugs. Everyone was so anxious to hear about how Aaron was doing.

As we began Bible study on Wednesday night, I shared with everyone what the doctor had said concerning Aaron's eyes. Then I told them what God said to me. I told them that I had never heard from God like this before, and it was important that we do as God had told me. I asked them to please phrase their prayers in a way that praised God that He had already healed Aaron's eyes. Many praises were offered up to God for Aaron's healing during prayer time.

It was hard to leave home because I was immensely blessed by my time with family and friends, yet I longed to be close to Aaron again. When I got to the hospital, the doctor asked me to go to the lounge so we could talk. As soon as we sat down, I asked the doctor, "How are Aaron's eyes?"

His words will forever be seared in my mind: "Well, I don't know how to explain this, but there is nothing wrong with his eyes. I've been working with preemies for more than twenty years, and I know what I saw. But what I saw is gone. Sometimes the changes stop and do not progress, but they NEVER reverse themselves. I don't know how to explain it."

I broke into tears of joy as I responded, "Well, I know how to explain it." He was listening. I shared about pouring my heart out to God and how God spoke so clearly to me. He responded, "Well, that must be it because I have no other explanation."

As I write Aaron's story of his miraculous birth and of his healing, it still brings tears of joy and praise to God. It has been almost forty-four years since Aaron's birth. Throughout this time, Aaron has been a blessing in our life that we could never have imagined. Aaron and his wife will celebrate their twentieth wedding anniversary this fall, and they have two wonderful children. All of them know Jesus as their Savior and Lord. They are faithful to worship gatherings and to being a servant for God. Let me ask you: Does it get any better than that? God is good and worthy of praise.

Do Ya Wanna Go to Germany?

For our entire marriage, we dreamed of settling down in Maine. As it turned out, we only lived there for less than two years after we married in 1978. It was financially difficult to make ends meet in Maine. Good-paying jobs were not as available as they were in my home state of Washington, so we moved back to my hometown.

Fast-forward a couple years, and we found ourselves in excellent-paying jobs with good benefits as civilian employees for the Department of Defense. We settled into our jobs, a home church, and made our first home purchase in 1984.

We were very thankful for our jobs, and we began building friendships at our church. We were eager to get involved in the church and found ourselves enjoying many different ministries. Our son was five years old when we began attending Crossroads Neighborhood church, and he was a young adult when he married. He and his wife began attending the church down around the corner where she had attended most of her life. I am very pleased to say that they are still active in this church where they have been raising their two children since their birth.

We continued to grow in our individual relationships with Jesus, and our marriage grew healthier as we continued to look to Him to teach us what love was. We enjoyed fellowship with the body of believers at Crossroads and soon found ourselves actively involved in many different ministries throughout our more than thirty years there. These ministries included Sunday school, youth group, young marrieds, governing board, deaconess, drama team, men's Bible studies, women's Bible studies, feeding the homeless, and various events designed for outreach to the community. These years were a time of healing, growing in the love of God, building strong friendships, learning God's Word, and experiencing how to love others.

I clearly remember being at work when my husband called. He said, "Do you want to go to Germany?"

I thought I must have heard him wrong, so I responded, "What? What are you talking about?"

He explained that one of his colleagues had been hired for a position in Germany, and they told him that they were looking for more human resource specialists. She asked if he might be interested. He told her, "Let me call my wife and see what she thinks." In my wildest imaginations of the adventures that God might take us on, I never considered it might be going to Europe!

As we talked it over with one another, we came to the conclusion that God was opening a door we didn't even know was a possibility. We decided to move in this direction. Well, it wasn't long before Doug received the job offer. It was a whirlwind of getting ready to move overseas began. We were living in a large beautiful home in a quiet neighborhood. There was so much to do: pack the items we wanted to take; put the items we wanted to leave in a storage unit; give away the items we no longer needed; sell the house (yeah, that was a big deal!); find a home for our beloved Golden Retriever; and the hardest of all, tell our son we were moving to Germany!

The sorting and packing was exhausting but doable, and we pushed our way through it quickly. The housing market at the time was not a seller's market. We contacted our friend who had been our realtor and told him, "We need to sell the house, and it needs to sell within four weeks!" He gasped. He told us that the current average time for a place to sell in our location was about six months. Then he said, "I can't do it, but I know someone who can."

It was painfully difficult to think of leaving our only son, Aaron. At the time, he was eighteen years old and living in Seattle. He was working for Microsoft and doing well. When we told him that we were moving to Germany, he exclaimed, "You can't leave me!" I lovingly reminded him that he left us first when he took the job and moved to Seattle. He said, "Yeah, but that's just a ferryboat ride away. You're going halfway around the world!" It was hard for all of us.

The comforting factor was that he was on his dad's orders up until he turned twenty-three years old. So he could decide anytime before that to come to Germany and live with us. Being on his dad's orders also gave him a family-member preference for jobs.

Finding a home for our much-loved golden retriever, Bridget, was very important to us. We decided that the best fit for her would be with my brother who lived in Oregon. It would be a perfect place for her. He was very ill, and Bridget was very much a service dog by nature; although she had never been trained. She obeyed commands the first time, every time. She was sensitive to how people around her were feeling and would respond with providing comfort to them. She learned quickly and always sought to please. She had a calm nature and was a great snuggle buddy. She never barked. She was perfect for my brother. We were greatly comforted with our decision, and my brother was excited to have Bridget to become part of his family. It was a match made in heaven! Bridget was the therapy that he needed, and he was completely in love with her.

The time came to get to the Sea Tac airport and fly out for Germany. It was a tearful farewell. I cried as I missed Aaron, my mom and dad, my family, our church family, and our beloved Bridget. I began to wonder why I had ever agreed to do such a dumb thing. Why on earth would I leave so many that were precious to me?

Oh yeah, our home needed to sell quickly. Remember how our friend and agent said he couldn't sell it in four weeks, but he knew someone who could? He was referring to God. One hour before we needed to catch the ferry to go to Seattle, he called and asked us to come by his office on the way and sign paperwork on the offer that was made on our house. It was a good offer. We signed and headed straight for the ferry. He was right, only God could do that in a housing market that was not in our favor. God is good.

Germany? In all my life, I'd never been farther from Washington State than Idaho, and that was only for one weekend. I really had no idea what I was agreeing to at the time, but I told my husband, "Yes, let's go." Time would tell of the challenges that I would face.

I learned a little German in third grade. We sang "O Tannenbaum." I remember thinking it sounded so funny. Well, that little bit of German was no help to me at all when I found myself surrounded by this funny language. I felt so isolated because I could not communicate. I was also in between jobs, so I was home all day, alone, while my husband was working. It made for a very lonely time. I was nervous about leaving the hotel room because (1), I could not speak German, and (2) I did not know my way around. I bought the *German in Ten Minutes a Day* book and tried my best to put some sentences together that might be of practical help. "The dog is under the table" was not going to get me far.

As time went on, we built a friendship with the hotel owner, Sylvester Vinegartner. With the help of his head cook who spoke a little English, we were able to have some satisfying communication. We would later discover that he was somewhat of the town godfather! He was well-known and respected. This would become very clear when it came time for us to find a place to rent.

Just down the lane from his hotel was an apartment for rent. We made arrangements to see it. It was on the top floor of the building, and it looked out over the Neckar River on one side and over the rooftops of homes and the church steeple. We really liked it and wanted to make it our home for the next three years. The landlord had a property manager through the bank that handled his rental. We did not understand at the time, but a three-year lease agreement was considered a short timeframe to Germans. They preferred a tenant would agree to ten to fifteen years. Yikes! They apparently did not understand that Americans came initially for a three-year work tour with the possibility of extending for two years, but to stay longer was just not the norm.

The bank lady advised the landlord to not rent to us because we were not staying long enough. When word got to us that we were rejected for this reason, I was very upset and began to cry. I was in the hotel lobby at the time. When Herr Vinegartner saw me crying, he was very concerned. He asked his head cook to come out and translate so he understood what was happening. When he heard the story, he decided he would take care of us. He asked us to follow him to the bank where he would talk with the bank lady and make things right.

Before he walked into her office, he looked at us and said, "*Alles gut.*" That means "All is good." He was going to fix it. He walked into her office and shut the door. He was in there for less than five minutes. He came out and announced to us, *"Alles gut."* He had fixed the issue. To this day, I wonder what he said to her. Whatever it was, it was clear that his influence made a difference! He had come to know us as friends, and from that day forward, we enjoyed a wonderful friendship even in spite of the language barrier. God blessed us with this friendship with Sylva (the nickname he had us use). We came to not just like Sylva but to love him. Because we loved him, we wanted to know if he knew Jesus.

One night he wanted to take us to dinner at his friend's pub. On the way there, my husband and I did our best to piece together the message to Sylva that Jesus loved him. He nodded a confirmation that he understood what we were saying. We had purchased a book written in German; it was called *The God of a Second Chance.* We thought this would make sense to him since he had a bad heart and had experienced heart attacks and surgeries. He openly received the book from us and expressed to us that he appreciated our love for him. To this day, we do not know if Sylva came to know Jesus as his personal Savior. We do know that we shared of the love of Jesus for him.

Sylvester Vinegartner was a successful businessman. He had actually written music for Broadway. He owned a beautifully designed, furnished, and decorated hotel from an old tobacco barn. In the world's eyes, he was very successful. It has been more than twenty years ago now that we first met Sylva. We speak of our times with him now and then, and it always brings a smile to our face. It was a blessing to have the opportunity to share the love of Jesus with him in both word and deed for the three years we lived down the road from him.

It is our hope that Sylva came to a decision to place his faith in Jesus as his Savior and Lord. We love our friend and desire to see him again and enjoy forever with him. I never imagined that I would encounter a journey such as we had with Sylva. I will always remember this man and how God provided an incredible adventure in sharing the love of Jesus with this man.

My Last Time with Mom

I miss Mom every day. I miss our deep conversations about God. I miss her always being able to make me feel valued, wanted, cared for, deeply loved. She encouraged and challenged me in my faith walk. No matter what I was going through, my mom was always ready to listen, to provide comfort and words of wisdom to help me. Mom was called home to be with God a little after 5:00 a.m. on January 26, 2009. I want to tell you about my last visit with my mom. It was amazing.

She was on hospice care in the nursing home. She had been there for about two and a half years. A fall at her home put her in the hospital, and then the nursing home followed. I visited her often, sharing photos and videos of family, friends, and the beauty of God's creation. I put headphones on her and played some of her favorite songs. I knew she would never again be able to attend any family gatherings or immerse herself in God's creation. I read to her from one of her Bibles; she had several as she enjoyed cross-referencing when she studied. Little did I know that this would be my last visit with Mom in this world.

Her illness was ravaging her body. I still see her body position and her face so clearly, as if it were yesterday. She was lying on her right side. Her right arm was bent, and her hand was curled and positioned below her chin. The white of her eyes were gray, and she had a distant stare. She wasn't even blinking anymore. I had read the booklet that the hospice nurse had given me, so all these physical changes were what I expected and watched for. I took one her Bibles that she had in the room and began reading to her. I said, "Mom, I'm going to read you your favorite chapter in the Bible."

I knew it was her favorite because she had written in the column of her Bible, "This is my favorite chapter." She had also underlined verse 4, which read, "One thing have I desired of the LORD, that will I seek after; that I may dwell in the house of the LORD all the days of my life, to behold the beauty of the LORD, and to enquire in his temple" (Psalms 27:4 KJV).

On the other side of her bed was my dad, two of my brothers and their wives, my niece, and my husband. When I had finished reading this chapter, my husband said to me, "Honey, read to her from John chapter 14."

As I was turning to John to read to Mom, one of my brother's said, "She can't hear you, Marie."

I calmly yet sternly looked up at him and responded, "Oh, yes, she can." I continued and read these precious words from Scripture:

> Let not your heart be troubled: ye believe in God, believe also in me. In my Father's house are many mansions: if it were not so, I would have told you. I go to prepare a place for you. And if I go and prepare a place for you, I will come again, and receive you unto myself; that where I am, there ye may be also. (John 14:1–3 KJV)

The nurse had told us that Mom had not responded to them in more than twenty-four hours. No blinking, no squeezing of her hand when they asked her to acknowledge what they had said, and no winching, flinching, or furrowing of the brows that are indications of discomfort or pain. I thanked God that there was no indication of pain.

Let me tell you what happened after I read that scripture to her. She uncurled her hand, and with her index finger, she pointed upward, smiled, and had tears in her eyes. My heart leaped with joy as I shouted to my family, "Did you see that?" The only one who had been watching me was my husband. He knew what was happening, and he saw her respond to me.

I wrapped my fingers around my mom's finger and leaned in close to her face. I said, "I saw that, Mom, and you are right. You are going home soon." Then I recalled precious memories of times with Mom and how she always encouraged me in my faith walk with Jesus. I mentioned specifics and thanked her for loving me and never giving up on me. I knew she was concerned about her husband. I told her, "Mom, don't worry about Dad. We will take good care of Dad." Although I had told her that she was right she was going home to be with God soon, I did not understand in that moment how soon it would be. I kissed her goodnight at 7:30 p.m. on Sunday, January 25, 2009, and went home. I told her, "I'll see you tomorrow."

At about 5:10 a.m., my oldest brother, Harvey, called and woke me up to the words, "Mom is gone. Dad wants us all to meet at the nursing home."

Remember the brother that told me, "She can't hear you, Marie"? Well, he was grieving quite hard. He told me, "I feel so guilty." I asked him what he meant by that. He explained, "I told God to not let her just lay there but to take her quickly." I could see the pain in his face. In that moment, God provided the response that Richard needed.

I said, "Well, Richard, it sounds like you were in tune with what God planned to do." The look on his face seemed to be processing the comfort of knowing that it was God's will that Mom should go home to heaven at that time.

I greeted my dad with a long, strong hug. He and I walked down the hall together toward Mom's room. I was amazed to see her lying in the same position she was in when I left the evening before. It was in that moment that I realized how close to heaven she had been when I told her, "You are going home soon." It had only been nine and a half hours ago.

It was an amazing time to have had that visit with Mom and to know that she was very aware of what was happening. She knew who I was, and she responded in a way that astounded the nursing staff. They had watched her for the more than twenty-four hours prior to my visit with Mom and knew that she had not responded to them in any way: no nod, no squeeze of the hand, no communication that would have let them know she was aware of what was happening around her. This is how I knew it was a miracle from God: when medical people could not explain it, I could!

During my visit with Mom, I thought of specific times that Mom and I had shared that meant so much to me. I spoke to them in detail as I thanked her for loving me, for never giving up on me, for making an eternal difference in my life by being a safe place for me. I read more scripture to her from her own Bible; well, one of six that she used.

There are not enough words in this world to express the depth of love I had for my mom. Even when I took a turn for the worst and ran from God, she pursued me! *Wow!* If that isn't Christlike, I don't know what is! I was in danger physically, mentally, emotionally, and most of all, spiritually. Mom knew that. She knew I needed someone to come after me. When I say that, I am not referring to physically following. I am saying that she stood in the gap for me when I was in danger. She prayed; she wrote me letters and left them in places for me to find later. She invited me to spend time resting at her and Dad's home when I needed to get away from where I was living, from the wrong people in my life. She spoke words of life to me when I felt dead inside. She knew. God told her how to care for me, and He gave her His strength and wisdom to do that.

There is a song that sums up what I'm trying to say. The chorus goes like this: "Thank you for giving to the Lord. I am a life that was changed. Thank you for giving to the Lord. I am so glad you gave." Thank you, Mom. You let God flow through you to save my life. I will get forever with you to praise our awesome God!

Joel

When I was nine, my brother Joel was eighteen. I was playing with dolls without a care in the world. Joel graduated from high school and was out on his own. We were living in different worlds. I didn't really notice Joel much when he came around. I don't really remember why. Perhaps it was because he didn't notice me much either, or maybe we were each just doing our own egocentric thing. Whatever the reason, that's the way it was. The point is that we did not grow up together.

I would later learn that in his early twenties, he went to war in Korea. Our worlds did not intersect. Well, up until I was a teenager and in love with horses. At that point, I was very interested in hanging around with Joel because he had several horses, and it meant that I would get to ride. He was kind and took me out riding with him now and then. Although it wasn't as often as I had wanted, I was always excited when I got to go. Even at this point in my life, I was still very egocentric and am now ashamed to admit that I still did not demonstrate interest in Joel as an individual, rather only for what he could do for me.

I remember how I thought he was such a cool brother because he had horses, and he was really good with them. I did admire that about him. I also remember how kind he was in giving me chances to go riding with him. Joel understood my love of horses. For my sixteenth birthday, he gave me a colt. I was beyond ecstatic with excitement! My dream of having my own horse had become a reality. Again, Joel's kindness was demonstrated to me.

Many years would pass, and Joel and I would each continue to be busy about our own lives. He came to the house now and then to visit with Mom and Dad. He and his wife would also come for holiday dinners. I remember thinking of him as my hippy cowboy brother. He always kept his hair long and had a mustache. I thought he was quite handsome.

It wasn't until the summer of 2009, when Joel became very ill, that he and I would begin to develop a friendship that surpassed anything either one of us had yet experienced. He was hospitalized in the veteran's hospital in Seattle where he had radical surgery to remove the cancer. They removed his bladder, prostate, and a section of his colon. He had to have a colostomy bag. He was in the hospital at the same time our mom was dying in the nursing home in Port Orchard. He wanted to go see her, so we went to pick him up and take him to see Mom. He got up and dressed, and we got in the car to go. We had just pulled onto the freeway when he noticed that his bag was leaking. We immediately turned around and took him back to the hospital. He was never able to see Mom before she died.

When Joel was released from the hospital, he was restricted from stairs, so he could not live with us. Our sister, Nola, had a one-level home and was able to have Joel live with her while he recovered from surgery. After several months, he had gained strength and was able to move in with us. We both would soon realize that our time together was short.

Joel was never one to complain and kept a lot to himself. When the pain and blood in his urine first began, he did not tell anyone and did not go to a doctor. He allowed the pain and bleeding to continue for too long. By the time he received medical attention, he was in severe pain and the cancer had advanced to the point that they could not stop it. He woke me and Doug up in the middle of the night and told us he was hurting.

By the time we got him to the emergency room, his pain level was a ten! After much testing, they took him into surgery. Doug and I waited and prayed. I remember the doctor coming out of surgery to tell me and Doug that the cancer had spread throughout his entire internal organs, and he simply closed him back up because there was nothing he could do. "I'm sorry," the doctor said. I was overwhelmed with feelings of sadness and guilt too, for not having valued Joel so much earlier in my life. Now he was going to die soon, and I didn't have the time I now longed to have.

The next step was moving Joel to hospice. One day, Aaron and Larissa brought Isaac to visit Uncle Joel—or as Isaac knew him, the cookie monster. Here's the back story: Joel loved good cookies, and it was hard to keep the jar full. One night, Aaron, Larissa, and Isaac came over for dinner. As usual, the first thing that Isaac enjoyed doing was to run to the cookie jar to see what type of yummy cookies were awaiting his little fingers. Much to his shock and dismay, when he removed the lid to the jar and looked inside, there were no cookies there. He looked like he was going to cry. We quickly tried to distract him and get him to the table for dinner. He sat next to Uncle Joel. Before we prayed, Isaac looked at me and reported, "Nanny, there are no cookies in the cookie jar!" I tried not to laugh because Isaac was so serious and quite upset.

I responded, "Isaac, I think we have a cookie monster in the house."

He immediately turned toward Uncle Joel and exclaimed, "It's you! You are the cookie monster!" Uncle Joel tried to look innocent, but he wasn't fooling Isaac! He couldn't contain it, and his laugh gave him away. All the adults found it humorous, but I think Isaac was quite put out with Uncle Joel.

Now back to the visit by Isaac. Joel had a cookie lying on his stomach when Isaac came into the room. He hadn't been eating it because he was so sick. I whispered in Isaac's ear, "Isaac, go sneak that cookie from the cookie monster." Isaac giggled and moved slowly in stealth mode toward the bed. Uncle Joel pretended he didn't see him until the last second. Isaac reached up slowly to grab the cookie, and the second he touched it, Uncle Joel grabbed Isaac's hand and said, "Hey, what are you doing?" Isaac was surprised and jumped back. Uncle Joel grinned, giggled, and then held the cookie out for Isaac. It was the sweetest expression of love from Uncle Joel for Isaac.

Tears welled up in my eyes. It was amazing that Joel was able to muster up enough alertness and energy to play with Isaac, considering it was only a couple days before his body would succumb to the cancer. Isaac was just three months from his fifth birthday. Joel enjoyed Isaac, and Isaac enjoyed Uncle Joel, a.k.a. the Cookie Monster. The memories of Uncle Joel are vague for Isaac, but the time they had together will always stay with me.

Every day for the two weeks he was in hospice, family and friends came and went. There was hardly a time when there was not at least four or five people in his room at the same time. It felt to me like too much, but I knew that people were expressing their love for Joel. We all knew the time was near.

It was June 6, 2010. Everyone had left for the night. Doug and I decided to spend the night with Joel. I had read the booklet called *Journey's End* when Mom was dying in January 2009. The booklet talked about the changes that would happen to a person's body as they were dying. It prepared me for what was to come so that I understood what was happening. I watched for those signs with Joel, and because there were indications the end was near, Doug and I decided to spend the night with him.

Doug slept in the La-Z-Boy recliner beside Joel's bed, and I curled up on the loveseat at the foot of his bed. I could reach out and touch the end of his bed. By this time Joel had not been responsive for more than forty-eight hours. His eyes remained closed. He did not show any sign of being in pain: no flinching, clenching of fists, grimacing, or groaning. I thanked God that he did not feel the pain.

Doug was fast asleep in the La-Z-Boy recliner, and I was asleep on the loveseat. We were both startled awake by a sound early in the morning. We both looked toward Joel and watched as he opened his eyes, lifted his outstretched arms toward the ceiling, and let out a sound that is difficult to explain. It was not a painful moan; it sounded like an expression of awe and joy, like he saw something amazing. He then slowly lowered his outstretched arms, and his eyes closed as his arms came to rest back on his stomach.

Doug and I both knew that something special had just happened. I hurried over to Joel's bedside. I asked him, "Joel, did you just see something we didn't see?" There was no response. He had a slight fever, which the nurse told me is common near the point of death. I put a cool washcloth on his forehead. I laid my right hand on the top of his head, and with my left hand, I laid it on top of his hands that were on his stomach. I began recounting the adventures we had enjoyed together over the last eighteen months that he lived with us. I thanked Joel for those times and told him that I loved him.

I then began praying out loud. I thanked God that Joel knew Him and would be with Him forever. I thanked God that I would get to be with Joel again one day. I thanked God for being with Joel in this moment. The nurse had instructed us that if he took a deep breath and then stopped breathing, this was common, and he might go as long as thirty to forty-five seconds before the next breath. She said to count, and if it was longer than that before he took another breath, to come and get her. Just like she described, he took a deep breath, and it seemed he then let the breath out slowly. I watched the clock. After forty-five seconds, I asked Doug, "Please go get the nurse."

She came and listened with her stethoscope. She turned to us and said, "He's gone." I had never before been touching someone when they took their last breath. It was an amazing experience to be with Joel in the final hours and to the very end. I count it a blessing to have been with Joel as he took his last breath and entered into the presence of His Savior and Lord.

Doug and I have a theory. We believe that when Joel made that out-loud expression that sounded like he was in awe, that was the moment when his spirit went to be with God in heaven. His bodily functions shut down a few hours later. That is not in the Bible, and we can't prove our theory; we just know that what we experienced in that room with Joel was a supernatural event, and it left us in awe while Joel experienced something we could not see nor feel.

I had asked Joel many months earlier to share with me how he came to know Jesus. I am so thankful that Joel had shared with me that he accepted Jesus during his teen years. He told me it was Merrill Cronk (an elder in the church) that prayed with him to receive Jesus. Between those teen years and Joel's adult years, he had strayed from his relationship with Jesus. It was during the time that he lived with Doug and me in our home that he returned to his faith and grew in his relationship with Jesus. He regularly attended worship service with us at Crossroads Neighborhood church and also enjoyed going with Doug to a men's Bible study every week.

I will never forget how only about two and a half weeks before he died, he insisted on attending church. He was so ill that he did not have the strength to get dressed. He asked us if it would be all right if he went in his pajamas. My heart was so overwhelmed and blessed by his devotion to be in worship service that I will never forget that day. We sat together on the bench in the back of the church, and Joel worshipped his Savior and Lord! It was precious!

I am so thankful that Joel shared with me that he knew Jesus. I didn't get much time with him in this world, but I will get forever with him in heaven. God is *so* good!

Travel Arrangements Made by God

It is the phone call you don't want to get, but at the same time, you do. You want to be told as much as is known about what is happening with a loved one. It's hard to hear. It helped us make the decision it was time to get on the next plane out of Crete, Greece, and on our way to Bangor, Maine. It was January 2014.

The last we knew, Willie was responding well to treatments and getting stronger. He had gone from being wheelchair-bound and not being able to pick up a cheerio to back to walking on his own and, in fact, doing so well that he was back riding his motorcycle, with the love of his life riding with him. The motor skills required to operate a motorcycle told us everything was okay. So months and years passed, and we had no knowledge that anything was going wrong. We would later discover that his wife had no indication that anything was going wrong either, even that morning as she kissed him goodbye and he went off to work.

The call came in early January. Willie's older brother, Bud, told Doug, "Willie collapsed at work. They life-flighted him to the hospital, and he is on life support." We were in Crete, Greece, and Willie was in Bangor, Maine. We worked with the Red Cross and got tickets. The next morning, we were on a flight to Maine. We wondered if we would make it in time. It was January, and we were flying through Pennsylvania and into a winter storm that had encompassed Maine.

When we got to Pennsylvania to change flights, we looked up at the flight board to read that our flight to Bangor was cancelled due to the weather. With hundreds of flights cancelled across the East Coast, and thousands of other stranded passengers, Doug stood in line to try to find the next available flight that would get us to Bangor, Maine, as close as possible, as fast as possible. What were the odds? We prayed.

I watched the bags, while Doug endured the long line while his heart was breaking. Finally, Doug was next to be helped. He stepped up to the desk and explained that he was trying to get home in a hurry because his brother was on life support. The customer service person did not give much hope that we would be successful in getting a flight soon to the location we needed. She directed us to another gate where we were told we could try to get a flight, but the odds were not in our favor. God had other plans.

As Doug stepped away from the counter, the man behind him said, "Excuse me, sir, I didn't mean to eavesdrop, but I couldn't help but overhear that you are trying to get to Bangor, Maine. That is where my wife and I are going. If you can get on this flight with us into Portland, our car is there, and we have room for you and your wife and your luggage. You are welcome to ride up to Bangor with us." *Wow!* If that wasn't clear enough that God was in control, listen to what happened next. The man continued, "So are you going specifically to Bangor or somewhere outside Bangor?"

"We are actually going to Winterport, to my brother's house," Doug answered.

The man responded, "We live in Frankfort, so we drive right through Winterport. May I ask where in Winterport?"

Doug replied, "His house is right on Route 1." Then Doug asked, "And did you say you live in Frankfort? I grew up in Frankfort!" The man and his wife shared how they moved there a few years ago with the desire to set up a small, sustainable farm. As he described where the home was, Doug knew exactly where he was describing. He identified old friends that he used to know that lived on the same hillside. Coincidence? Luck? No. God: that is what was happening. God alone. God in charge. God taking care of us and providing the way to get home to Willie and a grieving family.

Another challenge: getting on the same flight with this kind couple that has offered to drop us off at the front door of Bud and Melanie's home. What are the odds? By the world's mathematical probability and statistics? Not very good. There were hundreds of people all trying to find other flights out of Philadelphia. Everyone was trying their best to get an outbound flight in the middle of a winter storm. We made our way through the airport to the flight that was destined for Portland, Maine. The waiting area was full. We waited.

After a while, we went up to the counter and asked the woman what the odds were of getting on that plane. "I'm sorry, but I wouldn't hold out much hope. There are lots of people ahead of you." We continued to wait. We watched around us, and people began to get tired of waiting; they left to either try a different flight or get a room for the night. We continued to wait. Again, the lady did not give us much hope. We continued to wait.

After about three hours, the lady called our names, "Mr. and Mrs. Campbell. I have two seats left on this plane." Again, I ask you, coincidence, chance, luck? No! God. God alone. God in charge. God taking care of us! As we walked onto the plane and worked our way toward our seats, we passed the couple who smiled at us and gave us a high five. Have you counted how many times God has orchestrated our trip for exactly what we needed? Let's recount: first, the man behind Doug in line hears where he is going and offers help if we can get on the same flight. Second, we discover that the man and his wife live in Frankfort and drive right by brother Bud and Melanie's home. Third, we get on the same flight with this couple after being told there was not much hope. Oh, there's more…

We landed and loaded all our luggage into this couple's car and got on I-95 toward Bangor. It's a three-hour ride, so there is plenty of time to talk. To say we were thankful for their kindness is an understatement! We began visiting as we rode. The man respectfully asked Doug what happened to his brother. As Doug began to talk about Willie, the man stopped Doug when he heard Doug say that Willie was an electrician with MMC on Mount Desert Island. "Excuse me, I need to let you know something. I am the manager for the life flight that airlifted your brother from Mt. Desert Island to the Bangor hospital. I was the one that called out the flight to respond to your brother." That's the fourth miracle orchestrated by God! When God is in charge, mathematical probability does not matter! We were speechless! How awesome is our God! The man proceeded with, "I may know more than you do about what happened to your brother. It may help you to know that when he stepped out of his vehicle, he immediately collapsed. He was most likely brain-dead before he hit the pavement. He did not suffer. From the time my EMTs arrived, your brother was on life support. He was not conscious at any time while my EMTs were there or during the fight."

The man's wife chimed in and shared that she knows our brother Bud who is a nurse at the hospital. "I'm a pharmacist at Eastern Maine Medical, so I interface with him regularly. He's a really nice guy," she says. No surprise to us; everyone who knows Bud likes and respects him. She added, "We are happy to help you." Finally, we arrived at Bud and Mel's house where they pulled into the driveway and let us out at the front door.

Some may call all this coincidence, luck, or chance. Let's consider that for a moment. *Coincidence* is defined as "a remarkable concurrence of events or circumstances that have *no apparent causal connection with one another.* The perception of remarkable coincidences may lead to supernatural, occult, or paranormal claims."

Luck means "a remarkable concurrence of events or circumstances without apparent causal connection."

The last one, *chance,* is defined as "the occurrence and development of events *in the absence of any obvious design.*"

There were *obviously* events that were directly related to one another, so that rules out coincidence. There was *obviously* a connection of events, so that rules out luck. For all of these events to occur at the precise location and time that we needed certainly shows an *obvious* design. Events were perfectly aligned, in time and location, for precisely what we needed. Every event fell perfectly in place to get us home and did so with the added miracle of connecting us with the man who had called the airflight for Willie. There was *obvious* design every step of the way in this true story.

My husband and I don't call it coincidence, luck, or chance; we call it a miracle of God. Order does not come out of chaos. God is the God of order, and He is the one that receives all glory and honor for these travel arrangements.

Too Old

I laughed. "That ship has sailed," I told my husband. I had held onto the dream for more than thirty years, but now it was too late. It was time to let go of the dream.

Doug insisted. "Why is it too late?" he responded.

"You've got to be kidding. I'm fifty-six years old!" I said.

He wouldn't let it go and asked me, "Are you dead?" He told me that if I'm not dead, then it's not too late. He asked me just to think about it, to consider it, and then decide. I did just that. It wasn't long before I was researching colleges and truly considering going back to college to become a mental health counselor. I found a college that I felt would meet my desires and, very importantly, was not too far from my son and his family. I quickly became very excited about the idea that I could actually pursue the dream I had held in my heart for more than thirty years.

The college that captured my attention had one word posted in bold letters on their main page. That word was *transformation*. I knew I had room to grow (even at my advanced age of fifty-six). I wanted to experience transformation. Western Seminary was located in Portland, Oregon, about a four-hour drive from my son and his family. Next, of serious consideration was the tuition. I was pleased to find that this too met my requirement of being within reach. I also wanted a counseling degree that had an emphasis on my Christian faith. So with the opportunity to learn transformation, be close to my son and his family, a tuition that was reachable, and Bible and theology classes as part of the program, it felt right. I had an excitement stirring inside of me with a significant amount of nervousness at the same time. I wondered if I would be able to be successful.

With the encouragement of my husband (and many prayers on my part), I proceeded with the application process. It was a joyful day when I received the email that told me I had been accepted to Western Seminary. I wanted to test the waters, so I signed up for only one course for my first semester. I took a Bible course. I was living in Crete, Greece, at the time, so this online course was conducive to continuing to work my full-time job and begin finding my rhythm of being a college student again. I had completed my BA in psychology in 2013 and was ready to work on my MA in counseling. I found the Bible course to be interesting and even fun. I had lots of questions for the professor. He was patient, kind, and always encouraged me. I looked forward to the day when I would meet him in person.

In April of 2015, I stepped foot on the campus of Western Seminary for the first time. I had an appointment to meet with the director of the counseling program and one of the counseling professors for the required interview. I was nervous. I really didn't need to be, as Kay, the director, and Dave were very friendly and made me feel at ease right away. I was able to share with them my dream that began many years ago and the reason that I've held that desire in my heart. It was a really great time sharing with them.

After the meeting, I made my way down the hall to the office of Dr. Carl Laney, the Bible professor. I knocked, and he said, "Come in." I stepped inside his office and introduced myself. His response was so kind. "Oh, Marie! It is so good to finally meet you in person." We chatted for a little while, and I was pleased to let him know that I would be taking in-person classes beginning in May 2015 (Spring quarter).

It still felt like a dream as I drove to the campus and walked into my first class. I didn't want to be right up front, as that felt a bit threatening; and I didn't want to sit too far back, as that might appear that I wasn't really interested, so I selected a seat about in the middle. Oh yes, it was all very calculated as to where I would sit because I was very nervous. As I looked around the room of students, what I noticed was that most of them were in their twenties. There were a couple older, but like me, they were the exception. The voice in my head asked, *What are you doing here?* For the first several months of being in the classroom, I struggled with believing that I was in the right place, doing what God wanted me to do. I'll be honest here: I shed many tears throughout those months as I battled fear and discouragement.

One day, the director of the counseling program asked if I would meet with her. She was aware of a particularly difficult situation I had gone through. I don't remember most of what was said, but what I do recall is that she gave me the opportunity to explain how I was feeling about an issue.

With tears, I shared with her what had me discouraged and ready to leave the program. She encouraged me to reconsider. She reminded me how well I was doing in my classes. She asked me, "Are you aware you have all As?" I was aware of that, but the reason I was considering quitting was not because classes were too difficult but because I had lost confidence that I would be a good counselor one day.

Kay spent more than two hours with me. She told me that in the particular situation that had occurred, she did not see anything wrong with the way I had responded. She expressed that she only saw this occurrence as a learning opportunity and not as my failure as I was viewing it. She encouraged me to take time to reconsider. Looking back on this experience, I am so thankful for Kay's time with me to listen, ask key questions to help me process the event, and encourage me to continue working toward becoming a counselor.

God was faithful to me as I continued with the counseling program. He was faithful in guiding me through more tough situations and allowing me to become more passionate for hurting people. Fast-forward from summer semester 2015 to December 2017. I graduated with my MA in counseling in December 2017. It was an accomplishment that I was not sure I would ever come to realize.

April 2018 was commencement. It was my dream come true. A dream I had held in my heart for more than thirty years. This graduation ceremony was the first time I walked for my diploma. I was so excited with joy that God had allowed me the blessing of attaining a degree in counseling that would provide me the opportunity to extend hope, healing, and recovery to those who feel hopeless, are burdened with sorrow, and who have not yet come to experience that recovery is possible for them.

Stepping Out in Faith

My college friend sent me a message to let me know that the organization where he worked was looking for more mental health therapists. This place was a Community Mental Health Facility.

My colleague shared his experience working there, the benefits and the challenges. He told me that the computer record-keeping system is quite robust and takes a while to become proficient with it. The clientele is also routinely challenging due to the extreme mental health diagnoses that this organization services. I remember asking my colleague, "Do you think I can do it?"

Without hesitation, he responded, "Of course, you can, and not only that, but you'll be good at it. I highly encourage you to apply." God used my friend to give me the push that was needed. I applied within the week and heard back quickly from the Human Resource Department. It was not the message I wanted to receive. Short story: The email told me that I was not being offered a job. I was disappointed.

Then God. God entered the situation and began directing. I soon received another email; this time from an HR employee who was new in the organization. Nathan explained to me that my resumé was placed in the do-not-hire stack. As he was going through resumés, he took time to review mine. He was impressed with what he read, and he wondered why I was not offered an interview. He took my resumé to the director and told her that it felt like it was a mistake to not offer me an interview. He asked her to review my resumé and see if she agreed.

The next email I received from Nathan explained that he and the director agreed that my resumé should not have been rejected and that I needed to be offered an interview. He shared that he felt the reason was that I was applying for a level 1 therapist position (lowest pay), and I had a master's degree, which qualified me for a level 2 therapist position (higher pay). I love what he said, "Marie, I know there is something different about you and that the money is not an issue with you. I think you want to be here because you want to offer help, and that is what is important to you. They should not have decided for you. Would you like an interview?"

That is when I knew God was moving. I didn't yet have the entire picture of how, but I knew that God was in this!

I was excited and nervous as I met the board for my interview. My husband's advice before I went: "Just be yourself. I'm praying while you are there." What a sweetheart! *Love him!*

I stepped into the room and saw three managers sitting at the table. They welcomed me, introduced themselves, and asked me to say a little about myself. The questions began, as they took turns asking them. I took a breath before opening my mouth to answer and then gave my response. As the process continued, I was noticing that one of the men seemed to be much more engaged with me than the other man and the woman. Al made good eye contact with me, he thanked me for my answers, and he smiled. He was different. I would discover later why he stood out to me.

I received the phone call extending a job offer to me and asking me when I could start! I was excited, yes, and still nervous. I was told that I was assigned to work on Al's team. My heart leaped, as I knew there was something different about this man. He welcomed me and introduced me around. He showed me my desk. He explained the orientation training that I would receive and showed me the room to go to for that. We went back to his office and talked more about how things worked there and what to expect for a caseload.

As we talked, I felt free to tell him that I had sensed he was different. As we talked, he shared that he is Christian! I knew it! I shared with him that I am a Christian too! He expressed that he had the sense about me that I was different, and he specifically asked for me to be on his team! God is amazing. He orchestrated all of this. I later learned that Nathan is also a Christian. He told me in person one day in the hallway that God had led him to look closer at my resumé and to make sure I got an interview. Again, God showed up and took care of me. He wanted me in this place. I had many amazing sessions with clients over the fourteen months I was there. Following are some of those stories about how God was moving in the life of the client and in me as I trusted Him to use me.

Tom

Shadowing other therapists was how the organization allowed the new therapists to observe and learn. The intake therapist let him know that I would be sitting in on the session to observe and that I would not be saying anything. She then asked him if it was all right if I stayed in the room. He and I made eye contact, and he responded yes. The therapist then explained to the client that she would be asking him lots of questions. He nodded to her. She proceeded with the questions listed on the intake form. (I later discovered that it was eight pages of questions.) The intake was scheduled to be completed by the therapist in one hour. That alone is overwhelming for anyone to complete, let alone someone who had a client they diagnosed with schizophrenia.

As the therapist proceeded with the questions, I observed his behavior. He would often mumble something, as if talking to someone who was not in the room. Then he would look confused and not know how to answer the question. He routinely used his index finger to rub behind his ear and then would smell his finger. Olfactory hallucinations are less common than auditory and visual. This client was presenting with all three of these hallucinations. He presented as overwhelmed with constant input by the hallucinations.

As the therapist continued, certain questions caused him to go into an explanation that he didn't do it; he didn't hurt her. As he spoke, it became clear that he had been arrested for assaulting his girlfriend. He kept repeating that he watched it happen to her, but he couldn't stop it and he kept insisting that it wasn't him that hurt her. As he spoke, I had a visceral reaction to the torment that I watched in this man. I felt the sadness as a heaviness in my chest. I left the room thinking about what I had just witnessed. I found myself praying for this man.

My schedule soon began to fill with the names of the clients that were assigned to me. I was surprised when my eyes landed on his name as my first client. Yes, it was this young man. I was assigned as his therapist. The mission of our organization was to (1) empower hope through compassion, engagement, and connection with the client; (2) to empower relief through effective evidence-based practices that promote skills and resilience; and (3) to empower recovery by building upon strengths and supporting individuals in their goals. As I recalled the behavior of this man, I found myself wondering how he would be able to realize hope, relief, and recovery. I felt overwhelmed with a mission statement that seemed to be quite a reach for someone so tormented by his hallucinations.

As I walked out to the waiting room to call this client for his appointment with me, I was nervous. I felt helpless. I also had fear. He seemed to remember me from the intake appointment. He was calm and polite through the entire session. He shared with me that he hears voices that tell him to kill himself and, sometimes, to kill other people. I had a mixture of sadness and fear going on in my body at the same time. I clearly remember quickly sending up a help request to God: help for wisdom on how to help this man and help for protection in case he heard voices that told him to harm me, as that was the reality of his mental illness.

Weeks passed, then months, and this client continued to come to his appointments with me. Every session brought something different, yet his hallucinations and delusions remained the greatest challenge. As time went on, I had become more relaxed around this client. He never did anything that made me fearful. In fact, he was always polite. He seemed to have developed comfort with me. I thanked God for doing that. I interpreted that as hope for this man and most definitely an answer to my prayers.

Then came a session that I will never forget. He came in, sat down, and immediately became focused on his cell phone. Try though I might, he would not engage with me. He didn't lift his head, and he made no eye contact with me. I tried for a little while, to no avail. I decided that we just needed to end the session and try it again next week. I opened my mouth to tell him that, and the words would not leave my mouth. At that moment, he put his phone down, lifted his head, leaned forward in his chair, looked me in the eye, and said, "I believe in Jesus." I had a physical tingle go through my body from head to toe. There had been nothing said by him or me about anything to do with religion, church, God, or Jesus. He continued, "But he's controversial, so I don't tell people. But I can tell you."

In that moment, I knew that the Holy Spirit was in that room with us, and we were on holy ground. As the conversation continued, God prompted me to ask him who Jesus is to him. He clearly told me that He is the Son of God and that he died on the cross for his sins. *Woah!* This is the client who had not been able to carry on a conversation that made any sense! I was in awe! He shared that he had a Bible at home and that he liked to read it. I had a hard time not crying with joy for the work that the Holy Spirit was doing in this man. It was as if an on switch had been flipped, and all of a sudden, I was having a conversation with a clear-thinking man who was consumed with talking about Jesus instead of being consumed with hallucinations. For someone with schizophrenia, emotional flatness is a primary symptom, yet at the end of this session, this man was smiling. *That* is a miracle!

I walked him back to the waiting room, where his mother was waiting for him. She asked me, "How was he today?" I shared with her what happened, and she began to cry. She said, "He's been praying a lot at home, and something is different. I'm praying a lot too." I encouraged her to continue to pray. She thanked me. She and my client walked out of the building. That was the last time I saw him.

A therapist is often left wondering how their clients are doing in life. I only know one thing for sure, and that is that in our last session, this man made it clear that he knew who Jesus is and that Jesus died for his sins. I went back to my office, still tingling and praising God for showing up in that session!

Billy

As I read through the eight pages of his intake form, I felt the feeling of disgust. His crime was one that violated another human being in the most personal and violent manner. He had been found guilty of two counts of rape. He served more than twenty years in prison and is forever on the public sex offender registry. That is a crime that can never be expunged. It also means that he is limited to where he can live, and if he is able to find someone willing to give him a place to live, the entire neighborhood will be notified that a class 3 sex offender lives in their neighborhood. His ability to go about his life after his prison time was severely limited FOR THE REST OF HIS LIFE.

I walked down the hall toward the waiting room to call this client for his appointment with me. I will be honest here and tell you that my mind was flooded with thoughts of how to make counseling with this client of any value to him. In the Community Mental Health facility where I was working, it was common for us to assist clients with help finding housing and jobs. How was I going to help with that with the record that he had? I was very nervous about what would come up in the session and how I was going to find a way to help this man and encourage him.

I called his first name. A man began walking toward me. He was bald and had arms that had bulging muscles! He wasn't really tall, but with his other features, he looked scary to me. I reminded myself that I had not yet had a session with this man, so I really had no idea what it would be like to be his counselor.

We entered the counseling room and we both sat down. I don't remember all the details of what he said or what I said in that first meeting. I remember his tears, his downright weeping. As I observed this, I was praying quietly, *Lord, please help me to express your love and hope to this man.*

As I walked him out at the end of our session, he turned to shake my hand, and with tears in his eyes, he said, "Thank you so much. See ya next week."

I walked away, asking myself, *Thank you for what? What did I do?* It took me a while to realize that what I did was listen. I sat quietly while he wept. I sat in the sorrow. He looked up at me with embarrassment for his tears and apologized. People often do that. I just smiled at him and said, "It's okay. This is a safe place for you."

Months went by, and this man never missed his appointment with me. I observed that it was difficult for him to just sit and converse in the counseling room. I asked him if he would find it helpful to draw, doodle, or use an adult coloring book with gel pens to help him relax. He said that he would really like that. From that point forward, I brought the paper, coloring book, and gel pens to our sessions. I could see that this helped him to be much more comfortable in the counseling session.

I kept learning more about Billy as I continued to build trust with him. He spoke about his young daughter and how much he had let her down. He spoke of the mother of his daughter and how she told him he needed to stop coming to her house because her neighbors knew he was there, and it made them nervous. They wanted him out of the area forever. He had nowhere to go. He lived in his car and, at that, had to keep moving it from place to place so he felt safe. He told me he never slept well because he was afraid someone who knew what he had done would find him and kill him. He felt he had to keep moving to save his life.

I tried to get him into a housing shelter. I tried a few. Guess what? None of them took in level 3 sex offenders. He was in good health, and he wanted to work. I was looking forward to helping him find a job. He told me nobody would hire him because of his felony record. Well, he didn't know that I had a list of employers who hired people with a felony record. I excitedly showed up at one of our sessions with a list in my hand. I shared the list with him. He handed it back to me and said, "But what you don't understand is that they won't hire someone when their felony is a sex crime." My heart sank. I wasn't sure if he was right, so after the session, I talked with my supervisor. He confirmed what my client had said. Nobody wanted a sex offender in their organization.

After a few months, the client shared that he believed in God. He expressed that he wanted to attend church and had one in mind, but the fear of people finding out about him was too much to handle. I encouraged him to continue to pour out his heart to God and to remember how much he is loved by God.

The day came for me to have my last session with this client. I had prepared him for four weeks that this time was coming. I was moving to the East Coast. In our last session, the client was tearful and shared with me how God had used me to help him so much. I was overwhelmed with gratefulness to God for allowing me to be there for this man who wanted and needed an encouragement of a type that cannot be offered by the world. Because he wanted to talk about God and his faith, it had opened the door for conversations that reached through so much pain and had touched his heart. How do I thank God for that? I have found the answer to that: keep on extending His love.

Cody

This man was a client that was transferred to me because his therapist was promoted to another position. I scanned through his intake to begin to get familiar with this person. As usual, there were categories on the intake that would jump right off the page at me: murder. This man was convicted and served more than thirty-five years in prison. I had a visceral reaction when I read that. Intake forms on clients often evoke a visceral reaction. I could not think of one much more frightening than murder.

I met with the therapist who was transferring this client to me to receive some insight into the best therapeutic approach. Brad assured me that while this client sounded like someone to be fearful of on paper, he was one of the most gentle and polite clients he had worked with. He told me that he is also quiet and has a hard time just sitting and talking. He said he is an expert chess player. If you knew how to play chess, take the game board into session with you and offer it to him. It helps him to relax if he can play.

I walked out to call this first client. A tall, thin man walked toward me. He looked timid and tired. I greeted him and led him into our session room. He was not the visual I had developed in my mind of a person to fear. He was soft-spoken and polite, a man of few words. I could only imagine the hell he had been through while in prison. He never told me the story of the murder, and I never asked. All he offered was this: "I did it. I was guilty. I'm not sorry I went to prison because that is where I met Jesus." WOAH! WHAT? All of a sudden there was a peace in the room that came over me. The Holy

Spirit was present, and it was amazing! Cody shared about various times in his life when God helped him and blessed him.

I surprised him and pulled the chess game out of my bag. "Would you like to play chess?" I asked.

His face lit up, and he responded with excitement. "Sure, do you play?"

I told him, "Yes, but I'm not any good."

He said, "That's okay. I'll teach you." This man told me about how he had plenty of time to study chess while in prison, and he had become known as the chess champion for most of his years served. He would tell me about chess history that dated back to the sixteenth century: the names, dates, and who beat whom with what type of play. He was a walking, talking encyclopedia on chess!

A few months passed. One day we were playing, and I just completed my move. As I took my hand off my piece, I announced, "Check."

He responded, "You might want to look at that again." I was thinking I had made a big mistake and put my queen in danger. I didn't see it. "That's not check. That's checkmate!" he said. For those who may not know chess terms, that means I had just beaten the chess champ!

I looked him in the eye and said, "Wow! You are a really good teacher!" I wish I could have bottled the expression of happiness on his face.

I saw this client for about eight months. We played chess in most sessions; I did not ever expect to play well enough to win. I won twice. That was two times more than I would have ever thought possible. We had a good laugh both times: me because I was shocked I had won, and him because he was pleased that I was learning from him. Out of the fifty clients on my caseload, this man was the easiest going and most pleasant of all. I learned to not judge by paperwork. The past of people is not a guarantee of what they are like in the present. I think of Cody now and then, and a smile breaks out across my face.

Moving to Maine

We had dreamed of living in Maine for a long time. On every visit, we would look at real estate and dream of making it come true. The hope was that it would happen sooner than later so that our son would grow up in Maine. Well, it came later. Much later. Like forty years later!

The day drew closer in May of 2019. At that time, I was working at a Community Mental Health facility in Lakewood, Washington. It was the most challenging and rewarding counseling position I had ever experienced. It was both exciting and sad to wrap up my time there and say goodbye to the friends I had made there. We were living on campus at a rescue mission where Doug provided a security service, and I offered counseling to the residents.

It was time for Doug to give our notice there as well and prepare to say our goodbyes. He had enjoyed his ministry of being available to watch over the safety and well-being of the women and children that lived at this rescue mission. For some, he was like a big brother ready to help, a father ready to provide wise advice, a teacher who offered much-needed education, and a grandpa to the children. He was deeply loved and appreciated by the residents and the staff. It was a tearful time for him to say goodbye.

We decided that the most financially smart way to do our cross-country move was for us to rent a moving truck and car carrier that Doug would drive across while I was completing my last days at my job. He was like a horse to the barn and made the trip in three and half days! *Wow!*

He flew back to Washington state, and after a few days of recovery, we loaded our truck with the last of our clothes and other necessities. We enjoyed the beauty of our cross-country trip as we touched many states that we had not yet been in. We arrived on June 16, 2019.

We started our new life together in Maine, but Maine was not home for me. Not yet.

The reality of being so far from my son and his family and lifetime friends hit me with an avalanche of emotions that seemed to bury me. The cabin was cute and provided all we needed. His family was kind and helpful. It was a beautiful setting. All appeared to be good on the outside, but inside, I felt like I was dying. I'd left my son and his family—my only son and my only grandchildren. I'd left my church, my friends, the familiarity of knowing my way around. I cried a lot. I wondered if I was going to find contentment in light of all I had lost. I was struggling.

God had been speaking to me about my lack of contentment. My focus had been on all that I lost when we moved: close proximity to my son and his family, a home church with many friends, my mom and dad, brothers and sister, and the comfort of knowing my way around the area.

The Bible teaches us that we are to walk by faith, not by sight. For me, that means that no matter what my physical eyes see or what my human emotions are feeling, I need to choose to trust that God is enough to sustain me. He is enough to strengthen me when challenges come. He teaches me to choose His way over my way of doing life. He lifts me up and provides the contentment I need.

You see, in my weak human nature, I was basing my contentment on people, places, and things. I'm still learning and growing as God leads me. My contentment is based on my relationship with Jesus. Oh, don't get me wrong, I'm not saying this has been an easy lesson. I am saying that I am convinced that when I draw near to God, He draws near to me, and *this* is my contentment. *This* is where I find all that I need. Spending time in God's Word, in prayer, in fellowship with believers, and being active in ministry is how I grow closer to God and find that contentment.

Contentment

My contentment was found in having my family and friends close in miles. In 1978, I married a man from the East Coast. I was from the West Coast. When I said yes at the young age of twenty, it did not occur to me how much living away from my family and friends would cause me such heartache. Three days after our wedding day, we moved to Maine. I struggled with missing my family and friends to the point of tears. I remember the phone call to my mom one day, in which I told her that I wanted to come home. She said, "Honey, you need to grow where you are planted." Mom has been in heaven since January 26, 2009, and yet I still hear those words in my head: "Grow where you are planted." I didn't want to hear that. At the same time, I knew she was right. The next year and a half, we lived in Maine. I loved my husband, and my new family here was great; but I experienced a sadness and longing that I had never known before.

During this time in Maine, I became pregnant with our son. This was a major milestone that I went through without my mom close to me. Don't get me wrong, Mom Campbell was wonderful. She was supportive and caring. Her love for me helped me through this new experience.

In May of 1980, my husband and I decided to move back to Washington state. We loaded everything we owned in the back of a Ford F-150. We set my husband's motorcycle in a cradle on the tailgate. Our son was eight months old and comfortably sat between us on the seat. I was so excited to be going back home because that meant I would once again have contentment. I had still not learned that contentment, for me, needed to be found not in my physical location and reliance on people in my life but in my relationship with Jesus Christ. That lesson was going to enter my life again many years later.

We settled back in my hometown where my family and friends were physically close to me. God provided excellent jobs for us in civil service, and we were back in a familiar location with the people I loved; I was content again.

I had forty years in my contentment. The day of retiring from our jobs came. We had talked a lot about retiring over those forty years. We talked much about retiring to Maine, where our dollar went further, and we would be close to the Maine family. I love Doug's family and the beauty of Maine. I knew that, financially, it made sense. It made sense in all these ways, and at the same time, it meant once again I would be many miles away from my family and friends. I knew what it would be like.

It was an extreme emotional time for me. It was more difficult this time, as we now had two grandchildren. I now would not only be leaving my family of origin but also my son, his wife, and my two grandchildren. Another thing my mom said to me, and I heard it as if she were speaking those words to me once again: "Your place is with your husband." I shed many tears as I anticipated another move to Maine, one that I knew was intended to be our last move.

Even with prior knowledge of the difficult adjustment I knew what was coming, I had not yet fully realized how hard this move would hit me this time. I went through such anxiety and depression that I often took a walk just so I could cry where my husband could not hear me. I did not want him to know how much I was struggling.

Doug was thrilled to be home. We bought a place next door to his twin sister's camp where she and her husband were every summer. Doug was excited to be able to be with his dad too. He was in his happy place. He was content. I was suffering. I was not content.

One day, the pain I was experiencing burst out of me, and I told Doug how much I was hurting. Well, that was in the summer of 2019. It is now 2022, and the honest truth is that I am still struggling. Again, the lesson I must learn is contentment. I prefer closure to issues. I want to figure it out, solve it, and put a closure to it.

For these years, I have equated missing my son and his family with not being content in God. I found myself using a therapeutic approach with myself that I learned in college. DBT (Dialectic Behavioral Therapy) teaches that two facts that seem to be in conflict can be true at the same time. It is a common reaction (which I had) to think it is necessary to choose one or the other. In fact, it is not about choosing: it is about learning to recognize and accept that both are true at the same time. I can give myself permission to miss my son and his family to the point of tears *and* be content in God here in Maine. That is a hard lesson, and frankly, one I am still working on with God's help.

The experiences I have gone through and am going through and will go through are shaping me. God is not following the script I handed Him. This is where the rubber hits the road, so to speak. If I say that I trust God, then am I willing to relinquish my plan for His? Ouch. That is a question that involves deep soul-searching. It is a question that continues throughout my lifetime as God challenges me and shapes me to be less like me and more like Him.

About the Author

Marie Campbell is a follower of Jesus Christ. She is passionate about her faith and sharing with others how Jesus has worked in her life throughout the years. She shares her encounters with Jesus to encourage others in their faith walk.

www.ingramcontent.com/pod-product-compliance
Lightning Source LLC
Chambersburg PA
CBHW041651150726
48005CB00013BA/1612